MAY I SAY NO

Also by Gregory Woods from Carcanet

We Have the Melon

GREGORY WOODS

MAY I SAY NOTHING

Oliver,

— with thanks for your
presentation of my
paper —

Greg

Keele, March 2002

CARCANET

First published in 1998 by
Carcanet Press Limited
4th Floor, Conavon Court
12-16 Blackfriars Street
Manchester M3 5BQ

A CIP catalogue record for this book
is available from the British Library
ISBN 1 85754 384 X

The publisher acknowledges financial assistance
from the Arts Council of England

Set in 10pt Meridien by Bryan Williamson, Frome
Printed and bound in England by SRP Ltd, Exeter

For Tim Franks

'more objectivity, more passivity, more indifference, hence poetry'

(Genet)

Acknowledgements

Some of these poems, or earlier versions of them, were published in the following magazines: *Anatomy, Capital Gay, The Genuine Article, Onwords and Upwords, Parnassus of World Poets, Pink Ink, PN Review, The Printer's Devil, Screever*. Others appeared in two Poetry Now collections and in the following anthologies: Steve Anthony (ed.), *Of Eros and of Dust*; Peter Daniels & Steve Anthony (eds.), *Jugular Defences*; *The Forward Book of Poetry 1996*; Berta Freistadt & Pat O'Brien (eds.), *Language of Water, Language of Fire*; Michael Lassell (ed.), *Eros in Boystown*; and David Laurents (ed.), *The Badboy Book of Erotic Poetry*. I am grateful to Pink Ink, Nottingham's gay writing group, for support and encouragement.
When the 1987 fire-bombing of the London newspaper *Capital Gay* was announced to the House of Commons, the Conservative member of parliament Elaine Kellett-Bowman was said to have heckled, 'Quite right! There should be an intolerance of evil!' Hence, 'The Fire Raiser'.

Contents

PART THREE

PART ONE

Orpheus to the Men of Thrace

No reason for a poet to be coy.
I recommend the taking of a boy

To lunch, to heart and, somewhere in between,
To bed. The ideal age is any teen.

No matter how complete he seems his youth
Will not endure. Develop a sweet tooth:

A boy will give you no return but honey
And sticky inspiration. Take some money

For the reluctant are coercible.
Oh, and their bodies are reversible.

Warlord

Achilles grieves. A soldier, weeping, seems
No less the hero – still delivers dreams.

Not powder running down his face, but tears
In the dust. Not ardour in men's hearts, spears.

Who says Patroclus should have been a farmer
Or poet? Nothing left of him but armour –

Which is apt. Women should be kept as chattels
For bearing sons. Lovers for love and battles.

Men should philosophize and body-build.
They like to see their lovers kill, not killed.

Favourite

When Antinous poses, sculptors strafe
Him with envy. Their longing is unsafe.

They would readily spiral into debt
For a whiff of not lavender but sweat.

The emperor demands both boyish curves
And washboard abs, and gets what he deserves:

His pet equivocates between the gym
And his divan. Reflection renders him

Beauty in the abstract, a kind of lie,
A copy of a copy. Quick to die.

Maker

He touches the boy, then touches the wax.
Each compensates for what the other lacks,

But neither is sufficient. Donatello's
Forgery needs an apprentice with bellows

To finish it. The boy's left in the lurch,
The statue in the chancel of the church.

(Identical.) He looks as soft as swan's
Down. But he's cold, immortal, made of bronze.

The sculptor comes to see him, sees him, seizes
The day, ventures to touch him, touches. Freezes.

Rimbaud in Harar

I used to have the kind of body men
Would sell their souls for, and was heartened when

One did. A bourgeois poet gave me dosh
For licking me (I never used to wash)

And for the things I wrote. To tell the truth
I merely simulated the uncouth

But he was mesmerized. He loved my verse,
My arse, my filthy turn of phrase and, worse,

My bullet wound. Well now I'm out of harm's
Way, writing nothing, sozzled, selling arms.

Domestic

In the biographies they call my heart's
Desire my servant. But his private parts

Meant more to me than any public rôle.
Our masquerade demanded self-control

Beyond our capabilities, and yet
My guests were taken in – as etiquette

Required. (Tchaikowsky leads a modest life:
He makes do with a servant for a wife.)

Less than a retinue, more than a son.
It's true I paid him. Doesn't everyone?

Nothing

The chambermaid who made the writer's bed,
When asked in court what she detected, said:

'The sheets were stained in a peculiar way.'
My lord, what more could any witness say?

The evidence was there, in brown and white,
Of what the 'nothing' they had done all night

Consisted of. Unspeakable, now spoken:
The vessel of Victorian manhood broken.

The empire fell when Wilde defiled the arse
Of an Adonis from a lower class.

Another Wonder

1

The sight of him could not have failed to tease
The tender chisel of Praxiteles.

2

But he's maths's achievement more than art's:
His body adds up, the sum of its parts.

3

He flaunts his disproportionate erection
As if to violate the Golden Section.

4

He seizes it in one proficient hand
Like the Red Baron coming in to land.

5

He clenches eyelids, fists and arsehole tight
As if he has to come with all his might.

6

He breathes not a word, but a shape the word
Might take in order to emerge unheard.

7

Yet evidence of loving hardly lingers
Longer than the threads of semen on his fingers.

8

His presence radiates through cheap cologne
The finer essence of testosterone.

9

Botanic, fragrant as the hanging gardens
Of Babylon, his florid cock unhardens.

10

I cherish his pelvis, mother-of-pearled
With sperm: another wonder of the world.

Think, Feel

The tying of knots and insertion of tubes has occurred,
Effected with skill and a measure of brutality.
Between remembering and the anticipation of
Whatever comes, a breath of air on the expanse of skin
Might leave the indeterminate impression of a touch.

We are not given senses to prove a philosophy
Or to let a coercive religion exploit our lust
For guilt. You can't smell an abstraction, the philosopher
In the slot machine will tell you for free. You can eat shit
But you'll never be able to taste your own pragmatism.

Neil

He arrives without
expectations or toothbrush
but with half a smile.

He has nothing to
impart by way of gossip
or overheard jokes.

We drink alcohol
but as a formality,
politely relaxed.

Our conversation
fights shy of whatever might
give either away.

When he gets ready
to go I ask him to stay
just a bit longer.

When he says goodbye
in the morning I go back
to bed and to sleep.

I dream of someone
else, and when I wake up the
smell of him has gone.

Moment of Concentration

The ramparts are
howling. The sun

reeks of sweat.
Under the olives

cicadas are
seasoning the

afternoon. The boy
on the Vespa

unfastens his
shorts. (A lizard

skitters away.)
The solider his

place in fact the
more he quivers

in the haze. The
smell of him in

saturated cloth
evaporates.

When he opens
his mouth he has

nothing to say.
He wallows in

the dust like a
dog with an itch.

His muscular
thighs are sweating

like cheeses left
out in the sun.

Chambered

How one enclosed place
fails to live up to
the promise of its
artificial flowers . . .

. . . yet how another
though darker is as
welcoming as a
lover's 'Is that you?'

A Bed

I

My loving him is like a bed of nettles
    On which I toss and turn.
With heat as hot as Popocatepetl's
    He makes my body burn.

II

My loving him is like a bed of feathers:
    He comforts me to sleep.
He keeps me warm in all inclement weathers
    Because his down is deep.

Coming True

Having wanted him for
so long, inventing weak
excuses to phone and
    contriving

to bump into him at
the shops or out drinking,
having what I wanted
    I can't cope.

What I used to wet the
sheets dreaming of doing
I now do often at
    his request

and what I ask for in
return I no longer
have to beg the pillow
    for in vain.

How can I even think
of sleeping when I've just
exhausted any dreams
    I might have

had, yelping in the damp
behind his balls? Darkness
could never remedy
    this turmoil.

His Expressions

I want to say something
so funny it could crack
the solemn shell of his
    demeanour

and hatch that smile which no
one who's seen it can quite
forget, sleeping or awake,
    until death.

Yet since it is in their
plumpest seriousness that
his lips are also most
    kissable

when he smiles I ask a
philosophical question
in order to pounce on
    his reply.

Familiarity

Extreme, impersonal,
face to groin with barely
time for breath or quid pro quo
of warrant and request,
a tense polemic centred
on defiance – of fluids
not to spill, of pleasure
not to peter out before
its moment, and of lust
to satisfy desire . . .

. . . all this, this fantasy
of fact, embodied in
a plausible frenzy,
accomplished before sleep,
between sheets, early, is
resolved with an expedient
flurry of tissues
and judicious regard
to the necessity to
be up in time for work.

A Sign

I turn him round, pull down his shorts and slap
His arse. He crumples, laughing, in my arms.
I slide a finger into him. A clap
Of thunder sets off all the car alarms.

Solstice

First his navel, then the
heart-stopping shock of his
nipples and succulent
    armpits emerge,

their power to enchant
out of all proportion
to the simplicity
    of the event.

He hesitates, arms crossed
above his head, secure
in the canopy of
    his damp teeshirt,

unwilling to commit
himself, unseasoned, the
upshot of his display
    inhibited.

Meanwhile I plot my own
implausibly torrid
meteorologies:
    from where I sit

the coltish sun stays out
longer, the planet tilts,
the things of the mind go
    into eclipse.

Consent

Seeing your body spread
  Across the unmade bed
Beneath the light, no cloud
  Or cloth to dim its proud
    Defiance of the night,
    I revel in the sight.

As if some mythic creature
  Had set a trap of beauty
In each immortal feature,
  I feel the moral duty
    To fall for such a bright
    Incitement to delight.

If I were to refuse
  To render you your dues
Of appetite, and feed
  Elsewhere another need
    On other fare, you might
    Resent my oversight.

The trouble with attraction
  Is its demand for action
Regardless of the price.
  But here's my sacrifice:
    The passion you ignited
    Consents to be requited.

PART TWO

Henry James to John
Addington Symonds:
for it seemed to me

that the victims of
a common passion
should exchange a look.

They were thinking of
Venice, these kindred
spirits, gondolas

passing in the night.
One winks, the other
raises an eyebrow.

Reading in bed he
catches me unguarded
cherishing across

the dorm the maiden
blush of where his chest
adorns itself with

solicitous nipples,
and primly buttons up
his pyjama top

to the throat, his eyes
the more reproachful
the greener than ever.

A bed like this, adorned
like this, should be unmade
by the adored order

in his puberty,
the logical velvet
of his being undressed.

Grin and groin impress
my view of him with stains
and creases, keeping me

loving the self-love
he allows me here
only to endorse.

Crestfallen he folds
and breathless, distance
glazed into his eyes

like a pattern meant
for flower vases
meant for window sills.

Why so astonished
at this extravagant
outcome of pleasure

when the sun between
curtains finds his body
so balanced and achieved?

Tented together
against dryness in
our own tropic storm

we share a shower head
after the match, barely
aware of other bathers,

he letting me lather
his colonial tan
from neck to navel,

apartness lessened
by the tentative
daring of our cocks.

A little soldier
in dress uniform
listens intently

to Rachmaninov,
stroking his lips with
the back of a finger.

Two rows behind him
the poet can't wait
for the music to end,

the crowd to disperse,
the cultured killer
to go for a piss.

Gracious in his credit
a marine accepts
tribute of blow-job

defacing his nuptial
uniform against
the aquarium wall.

Having savoured the
conceded seed I
stagger off singing.

Is that in the smog
psychotic Capri or
an aircraft carrier?

Imagine a ship.
The bar across from
the quarantine house:

sailors in off-white
slur their remote words.
The one at the door

ignoring the rest
walks into the night.
You track down the gush

of his piss against
the custom house wall
and kneel in the wet.

Idyll

A vision has been granted me:
    A boy beneath an olive tree.
        I think, when I see Corydon,

That he's what eyes were made to see.
    He outperforms the bodies on
        The frieze around the Parthenon.

Who would have thought a boy could be
    As perfect as pornography?
        He turns on me. He turns me on.

Who would have expected
enough in the shine of his
elbows, seat and knees,

this tawdry Mormon, all
adam's apple and sallow
wrists, for anything like

an erection or poem
to come of it? Nothing
could save him from being

overlooked but this
goodly surprise: these signs
of contact with such grace.

Offer him a drink,
light his cigarette,
ask him to dance.

Tell him what you do
for a living, but not
as if it matters.

Ask his name and try
to remember it
for when you find him

knotted in your sheets,
a total stranger
begging for Aspirin.

When he stands over
me, legs dauntingly
apart, fists on hips,

I hardly manage
to prevent myself
flinching in dismay,

expecting his tackle to
come tumbling out of
inadequate shorts

as if a knife had
been thrust into the
innards of a pig.

You can tell he wants
you by the way he
has to wet his throat

sending his adam's
apple careering
up and down his neck

like the thing on the
test-your-strength machine
lambasting the bell.

No fluffy toys as
prizes but knowing
you managed the test.

There is a moment
when the lips before
settling in the small

of a boy's back meet
hairs too fair to have
been seen until touched

and hesitate there
as if discouraged
from going further

or amazed to have
been stopped from kissing
him seconds ago.

He undresses before
you ask him, eager
to get on with it.

When you say how good
he looks he doesn't
seem to hear or care.

He plays with himself,
hoping to galvanize
you into action.

He knows precisely
what you need and means
to urge it on you.

He comes to the window,
I can see him through
the venetian blinds.

He says the rain's stopped,
get up, come outside,
the trees are in leaf.

His voice in my breath
buzzes for honey,
dances by the hive.

I sit in his shade,
I am his he mine,
we eat in the garden.

The last time he shook
like this, racked by his
own frame, was on a

softer, broader bed –
but not in pain and not
held down by nurses.

Impaled to his guts
on the gibbet of
a merciless cock he

kept kicking out at thin
air, bucking his hips and
screaming – but for more.

Watching your lover's
body your delight has
thrived on for so long

decline into the
helplessness of old
age within a month,

when you consider
your own intact but
no less fragile beauty

where but in him is
what endures, where what
survives but in his flesh?

The drip-feed takes the
place not only of
the feasts he used to

share with pretty boys
in trendy haunts and
fancy outfits but

even the steady
flow of sentences
he couldn't do without,

sustained by every
hint of a rumour
and straining for more.

His old school photos
show ranks of athletes
with complacent smiles,

their hairy forearms
doubled in defiance
of the effeminate

on expansive chests.
He forgets their names
but his fingers recall

the glossy expressions
of those the game of chance
selected to die young.

He really believes
he's too beautiful
for it to happen

to him, too boyish
in the mirror to
lose his hair or die.

What would interfere
with skin so freshly
plucked from puberty?

Has nobody told him?
A thing of beauty is
a joy for eighteen years.

He's melting into his
bed, piss and more sweat
than you'd think a body

could contain pooling
on the rubber sheet.
His skeleton can't

carry its own weight.
Those perfect pecs and
abs have gone, leaving

the intercostals
like gunk stuck in a
grid in the gutter.

Inscription

I
This is to commemorate
    A moment which passed.
All the witnesses were late,
    The stonemason last.
What they made of what occurred
Could be conveyed in a word:
    Nothing.

II
This is to accentuate
    An all-too-human norm:
The living cannot but create
    Meaning in a storm,
But only the impassive dead
Can fathom what the thunder said:
    Nothing.

III
This is to anticipate
    The moment to come,
Fated to negotiate
    What we must become –
Beyond desire, beyond disgust,
Less than water, less than dust:
    Nothing.

Seeing him again
renews the nightmare
it would be a shame

not to have to survive
again. Having once
loved him is enough

to persuade me I
could still manage the
madness: purposeful

dot-to-dot kissing,
tears to dry, random
agreement/argument.

Not a lover but
nothing but love, you
represent nothing.

Part for part the one
and only perfect
image of itself,

your body suffices.
In bed with me you
keep it company,

too busy loving
to afford time for
the pursuit of love.

Your bicycle against
the wall, coat on the
back of the kitchen

door, your duffel bag
on the table, a
stubbed out cigarette,

boots at the foot, jeans
at the top of the
stairs, your underwear

on the bathroom floor,
specs on the bedside
table, dick in my fist.

The pony express could have
used you. No wonder I
play the cowboy on you

as vicious with the whip
as you allow. If we are
taken in by anything

it's believing truth to
life makes any difference.
My fake accent, your snorts.

Despite the sweat it takes
to make believe, we're not
as tame as we think.

I this afternoon
having nothing to
do, nowhere to go,

found my something and
its somewhere, between
two-thirty and four,

between a wall and
the sea, between his
hands, pernickety

but decisive, and
between you and me
neither of us was bored.

Not in two glossy
dimensions purchased
under the counter

not in clothing shed
all over the floor
of the locker room

not even in bed
a dream at the touch
of my own fingers,

only in person
at first hand only
naked only you.

Imaginary
lines between the stars
make the zodiac

obliterating
whole galaxies with
fancied animals

while on lines no less
flimsy you and I
establish the future

what matters not their
lack of substance but that
they are drawn at all.

PART THREE

Post Mortem

I
'All that the assassins have been claiming
has been lies. Their meetings were not social
but a plot. Each courted temptation
in the others' company: not one of
them was capable of acting alone.
When they shot the hero he was strong (as
heroes are) but weaker for being alone.
They had no pity, finding ample space
for all their bullets on his broad physique.'

II
'Call us good not evil. There's little more
to be said. We're men of the type, as you
well know, who counter vanity with valour
but pride ourselves on love. We seek glory
not in the dusty ruckus of the world
and subsequent damnation, but in God.
Spirit, intellect and theology
keep us going. Heroes, like lesser men
can meet with unfortunate accidents.'

Reagan at Bitburg
5 May 1985

An overcoat circumvents the globe, alert, attentive to
Seasonal effects – wind, rain, sleet – steaming when the sun
    comes out.
It passes like a homicidal mood, between elders,
Between the whitewashed marker stones, between showers,
    putting on
A show of dignity, passing like impressions through a mind
Distracted from maturity by game-shows on TV,
Passes and comes back, a souvenir, a memory without
A memory. The old man in the overcoat tries to recall
Quite what it was he once thought he was doing coming here.
The armed guard and the overcoat, together, keep him covered.

Yes, birds, clouds, martial music on the unreliable breeze,
Crowds kept at a distance, all buttoned up in overcoats, all but
A few old men in striped pyjamas, unaccustomed to the cold
But still able to remember and still able to resist.
The scene – yes, birds, clouds, music – resolves itself into a
    group
Of overcoats and stones, stones wire-brushed free of moss,
    overcoats
Newly dry-cleaned, the stones in rows, overcoats in step. The
    trudge
Of polished boots on weeded gravel stops, shuffles, stops,
    returns.
Nothing is said. Nothing happens. The old man in the overcoat
Does, or seems already to have done, what he came here to do.

Earplugs, music, shots, the past tense. Someone is shouting
    something
Somewhere else. The bandsmen go back to their bus for flasks
    of coffee.
The birds apart, silence or whatever you call it prevails,
Prevails over all but the birds, over the gravel, the stones,
Over the elders, prevails over the musical instruments,
The guns, the muzzled dogs, and over not the birds but the dead.
The soldiers wore earplugs to fire their salute. The man in the
    coat,
Faced with the dead, says nothing, has nothing to say. Silence
    prevails
Over the man the men are helping out of his overcoat.
No one writes him a speech. He has no one to say what to say.

Retreat

One would never come here expecting warmth.
The sanatorium on the far shore
is triple-glazed throughout. Nobody bathes
from its private beach; there's a heated pool
in what used to be the domestics' wing.

Even the bird bath at the meeting of
two paths is wired to the mains to prevent
the water icing over. Not that birds
are much inclined to winter in these parts;
most have migrated by early November,

not to return till after Carnival.
The topiarist labours unobserved,
whistling a Souza march to melt the silence.
His giant dogs and peacocks serve a need
for apparitions of the animate.

From across the water only the chimneys –
and only once the morning mist has cleared –
are visible, something man-made among
the conifers, perhaps a ruin or
a secret military facility.

We like elaborating on the view
our rented cottage dares us not to love,
giving names to the crofters and their dogs
as they pass us with no acknowledgement
(without a woof let alone a hello)

and making distinctions between places worth
the sweat of visiting and others which
are bound to disappoint – despite the fact
we've never been to any of them and
have no intention of beginning now.

The cold lake is discouragement enough.
There is a steamer which, as they say, 'plies'
the deeper channels for most of the year,
ferrying farmers and produce to market
or tourists to panoramas and back.

Its wake doesn't reach our slipway until
even its funnel has vanished behind
the next headland; but we have time to wait
for the wash to shin up the concrete slope
as far as our feet – or mine and your wheels.

The steamer also brings the newspapers
to this neck of the woods. Tabloids, broadsheets,
the self-important noises of the world.
We light our open fires with them, no less
to burn their hatred than to warm ourselves.

I hear things. Howling winds insinuate
themselves as much into the mind as through
ill-fitting window panes. You'd credit rumours
of rabid wolves among the rhododendrons
or torture in the drainage ditches if

you hadn't got into the habit of
earplugs by night and the radio by day.
Your bedtimes have encroached on our whole life.
When I lift you out of your chair you lie
against me as you did on our first night

when, having had more than enough to drink,
you had to stay both the night and the rest
of your life. There's nothing poetic here.
No nightingale to make us 'half in love
with easeful death', no lark to teach us 'half

the gladness' of its ignorance of death,
no miracle but staving off for one
more day the death of anything worth keeping
alive: the stones, the bird bath, climate, love.
Settle down to the routine of decline.

This Bird, That

1
This bird is an omen, that a potential meal.
We cleave to the conditions we could just as well
build pleasure domes against. The drizzle in our hair
is reassuring evidence of more to life
than setting minefields and extorting fortunes for
the maps. A small proportion in our midst look good
in uniform. We flatter them. We lick their boots.
They in return disdainfully acknowledge us
by starting minor wars for us to watch them win.

2
Relief is a matter of silences, desire
a shadow in the barrack room. From dead of night
to break of day the dreams we suffer from predict,
if we could only read them, personal events
years in advance, from sacraments to accidents
while crossing streets or climbing ladders, even slips
of the tongue that result in the parting of friends.
All screaming nightmares have to be reported to
Intelligence, the breakers of enemy codes.

3
In our own beds or in each other's we accept
our own mortality as non-negotiable.
Everything else is up for grabs: virility,
the etiquette of who does what to whom and when,
what kisses delivered in such-and-such a way
are meant to mean, and whether secrets we exchange
could compromise our national security
or only threaten someone we don't like with scandal.
Woken by birdsong, we shudder, unsatisfied.

4

Our pessimism hobbles us. We never fail
to see the fist implicit in an open hand.
The seven deadly sins have never seemed to us
much more than a monastic's sense of deadliness,
an eremite's aversion to the outside world.
Confessing them is like a child's 'I disobeyed
my parents' or 'I told a lie': the dozing priest
gives absolution in his sleep, our penances
are muttered in the street between profanities.

5

This bird is moulting, that is being plucked. The air
is full of feathers – breathable gingerly, just.
The children think it's Christmas and succumb to greed.
Their elder brothers strut about, more to impress
each other than each other's adult sisters, who
have better things to do than be seduced by bluster.
(They don't distinguish men from children: both need toys
and telling how to play with them.) The brothers drift
away. The feathers settle in the children's hair.

6

These are the entrails, those are giblets for the sauce.
The recipe is written on an envelope
as if it barely mattered. Improvise, it says,
according to whatever rule you set yourself.
The pots and pans will do the rest. The cooking smells
encourage salivation, but they soon go stale
in corridors already putrid with the stink
of paint and dirty socks. A rivulet of drool
dries out on each man's chin, unshaven, targeted.

7

To throw a punch to break a jaw you have to be
prepared to block investigations by the men
with lengths of pipe concealed about their persons and
a special line in threats. They aim below the belt,
these angels of officiousness. They always want
to know why anyone is laughing, who you spoke
to in the toilets, what the word is on the streets,
and what it is your body language seems to be
suggesting in the margins of the things you say.

8

Emergencies – in the event of which, break glass –
excite our sense of our importance, even if
our mothers thinks us all the more the boys we were
the harder we exert ourselves. The siren or
electric bell is suited perfectly to how
we think of our physiques as being built to act.
When in repose our sinews twitch as if wired up
to a corrective voltage, and our minds avoid
those thoughts that end up being spoken in one's sleep.

9

Whenever we consider hypothetical
catastrophes and what to do about them if
a weakened foreign government should call us in,
we ask each other leading questions like:
could seventy of us restore democracy
to an élite of cultivated Europeans
by taking control of the telephone exchange
and stopping any traffic on the airport road?
How many automatic weapons would it take?

10
On ceremonial occasions one of us,
but only one, is bound to end up naked in
a circle of the rest. Conformity to such
traditions – hands behind the head, legs wide apart,
some arbitrary token of absurdity
entangled in the pubic hair or hanging from
the genitals themselves, the very genitals –
cements the peer group and excludes the infidel.
We hand on what was handed down to us, full stop.

11
This man is telling us a dirty story, that
has had his right to speak revoked. We laugh at both:
discrimination is beyond us. This young man
is happy to attract admiring glances, that
would boot you in the nuts if you so much as smiled.
Because we find ourselves as unpredictable
as others find us, we can only guess our needs.
My right arm for a cigarette. My kingdom for
a mattress, someone else and cooling pools of slime.

The Fire Raiser

Two lovers stirred early, woken by streams
   Of light converging on the day ahead,
Back to their own identities from dreams
   In which they shared one body like a bed.
   Division was the focus of the dread
They tried with tight embraces to dispel;
But the bedroom window opened on to Hell.
     Said the Devil:
   There should be an intolerance of evil.

The moral arsonist came bearing light
   Into a place which, had she not been blind,
She would have found already lit. Despite
   The sight of eyelids she was locked behind,
   She claimed the right to preach to humankind
Her vision of a virtue forged in shame.
Her scripture was a newspaper in flames.
     Said the Devil:
   There should be an intolerance of evil.

She barged into the bedroom where the lovers
   Were watching daylight make their love routine.
She stripped their bed, she set fire to the covers,
   She shattered privacy like glass between
   Their bellies, moulding them to her obscene
Imagination. Though a word may hurt you,
None blisters like the blowtorch of her virtue.
     Said the Devil:
   There should be an intolerance of evil.

The lovers were uncoupled then and forced
    At gunpoint into cattle trucks, confined
Apart, and through a psychic holocaust
    Transported to an orchard just behind
    A bogus railway station. To remind
The world of sin, delight was crucified
On apple trees. All but the Devil died.
      Said the Devil:
  There should be an intolerance of evil.

(God, meanwhile, was trying to decide
    If he was on the Devil's side.)

Distraction

He wore nothing
but a leather waist-band, low
on his narrow hips, from which two thinner
straps descended,

one from either
hollow of his pelvis down
to the outer fringes of his pubes, to
meet at the point

just behind his
testicles, thence to ascend
between his buttocks to rejoin the
horizontal

in the small of
his back. The main purpose of
this contraption – other than to frame and
accentuate

his genitals
and effectively to bar
his arsehole – was to hold, suspended over
the left hip, the

Walkman with which
he protected himself from
having to engage in a lover's discourse.
On condition

that they didn't
try to unfasten the waist-
band or fiddle with his volume control,
his visitors

were free to roam
at will across the seething
snowscape of his body. 'Seething' because,
    from a forehead

overhung by
thick fringe to his sweaty feet,
he always appeared to be running a
    temperature – more

probably on
account of his taped music
than of the callers' strenuous caresses,
    judging by his

relative lack
of attention to the latter.
'Snowscape' because his body was evenly
    pale and hairless

all over – hairless
except for tufty pubes; white
except in the deep recesses of his
    groin, which blushed to

a crimson matched
only by that of his nipples
and lips. The visitor was not told when
    to start. Seeing

him standing there,
perhaps tapping his toes to
the music only he could hear, or flexing
    his buttocks to

the same, little
but the faintest gleam of his
eyes visible through his fringe, one had to
    make one's own move.

67

        Personally, I
    began by enticing his
apprehensive dick-head out of its prepuce,
        using certain

        inflexions I
    picked up overseas. I won't
retrace the courses taken on his flesh
        by my tongue and

        increasingly
    sticky fingers that morning.
(It was barely ten and the boy's breakfast
        was still settling

        audibly.) But
    in any case, by the time
he clenched his loins and sprayed my face with sperm,
        I had bathed his

        shins and feet in
    mine. Only then did I see
the empty cassette case on a chair next
        to the bathroom

        door. He had been
    listening – was still listening
now, as he wandered out past the chair to
        wash his feet – to

        a selection
    of songs from Walt Disney films.
I tried guessing, in vain, to which he had
        reached his silent

        climax. Some day
    my prince will come? When you wish
upon a star? Give a little whistle?
        Heigh-ho heigh-ho?

Going Somewhere

I first saw him on a tube train. He was standing at the door,
Trying to look sophisticated, scornful, sexy. Ears plugged
With music. I didn't see him till I saw him smile. His mouth
Oozed like peach flesh. I followed the smile down the carriage
     to where
A man in his forties or fifties was sitting, craning his

Neck, transfixed. They played the game of looking and looking
     away.
The smile came and went like ripeness with the seasons. Their
     timing
Broke: each looked when the other was looking away. At East
     Finchley
I stood up to get out. The boy got out before me. I followed
Him to the stairs. Just once he looked back to see if the man had

Left the train. I looked too. No. Didn't dare. When the crowd
     thickened
To go down the stairs I went right up behind him. We started
Down the steps and my left thigh hit his butt. To keep him
     from falling
Forward I grabbed his arm. People passed round us on both
     sides.
When I said sorry he stopped looking scared and went on down
     the steps.

Outside the station he turned right on the High Road and
     walked to
A bus stop under the railway bridge. He joined the long queue.
I stood next to him. I was thinking about his arse, wondering
If it would repay the effort. His jeans were cheap and loose, but
I could guess the shape. Pronounced. It was half six and people
     were

Going home, breathing winter breath. Our queue became a
    crowd
Before the bus arrived. I guessed an old man with liver spots
Would get in my way when the time came, and sure enough he
    did.
The boy jumped the queue, flashing his pass at the driver. He
    went
Upstairs, but I didn't get to follow his arse on the stairs

Because I had to help the old man on to the bus. He dropped
His stick. Someone was pushing me from behind. Although the
    seat
In front of the boy was empty I sat next to him. He was
Looking out at the end of the queue fighting to get on board.
I spread my legs so my thigh would touch his. I unzipped my
    new

Leather jacket. It was making me feel more confident than
Usual. I reached into my shirt pocket for my cigarettes,
Took one myself and offered him one. He looked at me quick and
Took it. Oily fingers with nails bitten to the quick. 'Thanks,
    mate.'
I lit it for him. We both knew our legs were still touching, both

Knew why. 'Where you getting out?' I asked. 'Where you like.'
    We got out
At the next stop and walked back to the station, bumping
    shoulders.
I had cut an appointment. It was for a Chinese meal with
Someone I liked. I would make it up to her another time.
'Were you going somewhere important?' 'Only home,' he
    muttered.

He was still living with his parents. Cypriots. I took him
Back to my place and opened some wine. By the time we knew
    each
Other's name we were down to our shorts, our cock heads
    touching through
Slimy cotton. We took it in turns to spit in each other's
Mouth. His armpits and groin were giving off a gamey smell.

He talked about Cyprus and the Greeks and the Turks and sang
    me
A meaningful song. I spat in him when he was singing the
Long last note. It dribbled down his chin. When I asked if I could
Eat his arse you never saw anyone move so quick. He was
Out of his shorts in a flash and lying face down on the bed.

He said he liked it best from men with beards. I arranged him so
His legs were apart and his cock was pointing down the bed at
    mine.
I looked till he grew impatient. 'Come on, man.' I slapped him.
    He
Clenched his butt and a pearl of goo squeezed out of his dick.
    So I
Hit him again. The cheeks were starting to blush. He hid his face

In the pillow. I hid mine in him. Straight away he was moaning.
At times like this I wonder what people would think of me. A
    man
In his thirties with his tongue up a nineteen year old's arsehole.
Just a moment of scandal, then I forget who I am. The taste
Takes over. How can you think of anything but living meat?

Skin

From 20-hole DMs
with toecaps scuffed as if
on a mendicant's teeth

to his No 1 crop
his menaces had the
effect on me he meant.

*

Like a colossus from
the floor, his eminence
had overshadowed me

before I reconciled
myself to the eclipse
of my humanity.

*

He suffered me to beg
for more of anything
he did I wanted less of.

I struggled to live up
to his command to be
beneath his dignity.

*

Not a word did I say
but what was given me
to say, and if I stank

I stank of him. As often
as he silenced me
he filled my mouth with filth.

*

Blindfolded, I was taught
to tell by taste alone
his armpits from his arse.

My licking him could well
have filled eternity –
like painting the Forth Bridge.

*

Extravagant, perverse,
he overloaded all
my senses with offence –

but I could taste a fear
beneath the sweetness of
his recondite tattoos.

*

When whetted torchbeams scraped
the shadow of his pelt
he ordered me to shut

the blinds. He had to gag
himself against the least
expression of delight.

*

Our progress left a trail
of telling evidence
discarded carelessly,

the instruments with which
he made the mark of his
superiority.

*

What became of the flesh?
There are no relics in
the quicklime of my heart.

When he left before dawn
the bedroom windows were
weeping like beauty queens.

Esprit de Corps

A partial point of view.
The buildings in the distance,
obscured by acid rain,

give the impression of
a garrison or jail,
a place to vegetate

or suffer in, where men
are subjugated to
the arrogance of stone.

On metal beds in long
unheated dormitories
where they solicit sleep

to put an end to boredom
but welcome waking up
from catastrophic dreams

their muscles quiver with
inaction, left unscarred
by unprovoked attacks

if none the less in pain.
The walls and windows stream
as if with tears suppressed

beyond endurance or
with sweat exuded by
a vague anxiety.

At dawn a filament
of woodsmoke rises from
the crenellated rooftop,

paler than the mist
the walls are hidden in.
Before the coffee boils

a bugle rips into
the buttresses, acute,
like lightning sent by god

to punish heresy.
Forget forgiveness here:
asceticism has

a habit of reviving
the memory of what
one came here to atone for,

if not in dreams at night
by day in other men's
perceptive ridicule.

The bugle sounds again.
Before it ceases each
half-conscious body, braced

as if to face its own
mortality, the hand
of the assassin or

plain accident of fate,
springs into passive action.
They do as they are told

as they were born to do.
Each has an oddity,
a mark or quirk it is

his only purpose to
conceal, his destiny
to draw attention to.

They do their buttons up
and buff their boots with spit.
Their recognition of

each other's dread unites
them like a culture or
a language but divides

like insufficient store
of rotting meat upwind
of the ravenous pride.

When marched into the yard
for air and exercise
they meet the mist with deep

suspicion, as if of some
contaminant brought in
from overseas on winds

unforecast but expected.
They lick their lips for traces
of poison (as lips are licked

in Restoration plays)
but taste their own unkissed
integrity alone,

no smile to compromise
the line their silences
conform to. When they spit

their spittle freezes on
the cobblestones. Their boots
strike sparks in unison.

Each treasures his tobacco,
his mother, his rank, one
perversion and one god.

At the End

At the end of the working day
when the sun is still bright but its heat

surprises you by coming not
direct but radiant from walls
or rocks or from the soil itself

when even the shade of a tree
is no cooler than in the glare
the hub of a crossroads gives off

where strangers sweat while trying to
decide which way to take to meet
or to avoid their destiny

and a breeze from the sea holds out
but breaks the promise of relief

inflicting up the river valleys
instead of more breathable air
waves of evaporated sweat

a man returning home from work
exhausted and scorched but no less
awake to possibility

than when he washed his face at dawn
and ate his breakfast by the pump
before calling his dog to heel

alerts himself to the precise
impression of cause and effect

in the complacent cherry grove
above a chapel partisans
set fire to in the civil war

where lovers go to make the love
that labels them and now a youth
with no such worldly need appears

the kind of figure you might call
a god if you had never seen
his like in pornographic films

or propping up the bar in some
disreputable urban dive

his manner all the more august
by contrast with the man who sees him
and does a perfect double-take

apparently as puzzled by
the presence of the boy himself
as by the way the faithless dog

bounds up to him and daring more
but fearing less than any man
before it licks his slender toes

a form of homage dogs devised
and men of taste have since refined

but no distraction intervenes
along two rigid lines of sight
between decisive frames of mind

the younger resolutely still
as if attempting the effect
a statue gives of restlessness

the elder swallowing to rinse
a throat dried out less by his thirst
than by the prospect of its quenching

his adam's apple agitated
by wretched inexperience

the sources of heat seeming to
have handed over all control
to little better than a lad

his sanctity attractive to
the anabatic wind by virtue
of sheer combustibility

the blush of sunset rendering
the very dust on his bare feet
alive with radiant energy

enough of it to make geiger
counter crackle like a magpie

and he the man takes him the boy
by hand along a footpath to
the spot behind a dry stone wall

where bullet cases shingle the
uneven ground and silence quashes
rumours of a coup d'état

the very place to place a boy
and in the dying light to strip
his person to its surfaces

recline it on the rusted earth
bare skin to bare geology

deploy a hand across each muscle
to offer to the dog to sniff
to send it off to fragrant dreams

then fold his knees up to his chest
and fuck him in the arse until
he sprays his distant face with ashes

which happens now as if again
and sends the man to sleep but not
for long before he wakes to find

a figure standing over him
unyielding hard-on in one hand

and in the other like the toy
the child he looks like plays with his
insatiable Kalashnikov

a soldier boy as much aggrieved
as gratified to recognise
in adoration his desserts

forgetfulness personified
or rather the most insolent
distraction from remembering

himself worth little more than the
occasional nostalgic jerk-off.

My Lover Loves

My lover loves me with kid gloves.
That is, no matter who's above
   And who beneath
   We use a sheath –
We never screw without a Condom.

He holds me in such high regard
He shields me like a bodyguard.
   Although love's dart
   Has hit my heart,
He fired it safely in a Condom.

Security is what we crave
To save us from an early grave,
   Our greatest wealth
   Each other's health,
Safely invested in a Condom.

Whenever he comes home from work
He brings me bribes, inducements, perks;
   But of his gifts
   The one that lifts
My spirit most's a pack of Condoms.

Although his clothes are always fine
(Comme des Garçons and Calvin Klein)
   He looks his best
   When he's undressed –
Yet even better in a Condom.

Among the catalogue of skills
Which generate our thrills and spills,
   His special knack
   Is to unpack,
Unroll, and lubricate a Condom.

Without the taste for being chaste,
We use a lube that's water-based
    And take great care
    Never to tear
The tender membrane of our Condom.

As long as he takes care of me
I am not scared of HIV.
    My lover loves
    Me with kid gloves
But loves me most of all with Condoms.

Landfall

I
The steersman, blithe as bones, detects
a rumour on the leeward breeze.
He follows porpoises, allows
the rudder to propose the course.

He turns his weathered face to face
a promise of indulgent boys
with purple feet and questions meant
to prompt outlandish narratives.

II
Their questions when you lean up close
are apt to smell of bubble gum,
their armpits of the chlorine in
the public baths. They laugh a lot.

Matters if not of life and death
at least of what passes for love
sit easy on their languid tongues.
Each knows the darker shadows in
his father's vineyard.

III
                    From behind:
they clamber up the terraces,

their agile rumps in trim, their throats
in training for such poetry
as might be needed when their mouths
come into converse with the earth.

A Blind Man Looks at a Boy

The smell of oranges – I could have been satisfied with that.
The spray – like an impolite but fragrant sneeze. I could
Have introverted all my senses, had I any sense,
And felt a thumbnail underneath the peel prepare to flay
The pulp. No need for an ending, no need to taste the fruit.

I could have sat here at my desk and been tempted by
All manner of profanities, my fingers dancing on
The blotting paper, sticky but as chaste as apathy,
The orange rolling on the carpet out of reach.
It would have been a simple life, a hive of discipline.

Instead the tilt of my tentative radar locates
A baffle at the centre of the room. My voice
Comes back to me a little late, diverted, each syllable
Coerced into the service of a boy's physique.
'Who's there?' reverberates on drumskin, naked abdomen.

A slight acoustic flurry, amplified within the vortex
Of his navel, makes me sound concussive, tremulous.
I seem to have decided – and been right – he won't reply.
The light is thick, life short, the stillness of the evening air
Transfigured by the delicate pomander of his balls.

Like a Shark's

We have the eye if not the will. The seasons attract us.
For every grove igniting lemons on a terraced slope
There's a fog; for every breath of air, air freshener.
Love has kept us occupied whatever the condition
Of the economy, no matter how surprised we are
We even like each other, let alone adore or worse.
We never learned to survive the pure menace of beauty:
Incisors like a shark's, angled inwards, no going back.

Reconciliation

If there were dancers, they were not dancing. If there was a tree,
It had not emerged from the rock. Potential was enough.
Fish, if there were fish, confined themselves discreetly to the dark
Angles in the shadow of the overhang, if the moon was out
For casting shadows. (Say, for the sake of the moment, it was.)

In the presence of the dust, we celebrated our return
To sanity. It was the dust we tasted on each other's skin –
You could say we made mud of it. Adapting our accustomed
Falsehoods to the requirements of the time, we reduced each
    other's
Serious intensity to laughter, an excuse for tears.

If there was a clock, hidden under blankets in a basket
Or thieved by brigands in the night, it would not for want of
    winding
Stop. We were reconciled to that. I slept in your armpit, dreaming,
If there were dreams, of you: *you* in the mountains, *you* on
    horseback,
You at the cash-and-carry. There was a sentence which recurred

In every episode. I knew it was the same but couldn't
Have repeated any single word of it on waking up.
Who said it, you or I or the kid at the check-out, was open
To interpretation. I think I spoke it when you woke me
But your kisses tightened on me like a buckled rubber gag.

The dancers, waiting for the music which their grace relies on,
Did stretching exercises in the mirror, not one of them
Indifferent to his neighbour's sweat. An earthquake or at least
A pompous thunderstorm could have served our need for an
    event:
Pylons struck by lightning, gigantic hailstones, children screaming,
    scared.

But above a crag surmounted by a dry stone wall, the sky
Did nothing suitably dramatic to confirm our mood.
The clouds were indistinct, the light uncertain. If there were
    trees,
They prospered undisturbed. If I shuddered when you clung to
    me,
It was because your hands were cold; if not, forget I mentioned
    them.

The coastguard's bell, the car alarm, cats on the fire escape, all
Made their token efforts and failed. The dancers retreated to
The locker room, affecting an impassioned manliness as rough
As the covers which slid to the floor, leaving us bare but not
    cold.
To the presence of the dust we celebrated our return.